An opinionated guide to

VEGAN LONDON

Text by

SARA KIYO POPOWA

& EMMY WATTS

Photography by

SAM A. HARRIS

Other opinionated guides to London:

East London

London Architecture

London Green Spaces

Independent London

London Pubs

Sweet London

Kids' London

Escape London

Eco London

Big Kids' London

Art London

INFORMATION IS DEAD. LONG LIVE OPINION.

Why buy a guide book? Surely, everything to know is available online. True. But if you are like us, you don't want endless information, you want well-informed opinion.

With the expert insight of Sara Kiyo Popowa and Emmy Watts, this book is an unashamedly short guide to the VERY best vegan places in this wonderful city, from fast-food eateries to ultra-refined restaurants. It is geared to both seasoned vegans and those more tentative. While it's not our job to tell you why veganism is morally vital, it is our job to celebrate that it's tasty, stylish and accessible to a much wider audience than many believe.

Since the first edition of this book came out London's vegan offering has gone from being surprisingly good to unsurprisingly brilliant. So often it's reliably better than it's meaty counterpart – fresher, more creative, more inspiring. This book is a celebration of that excellent trend.

Enjoy.

Ann and Martin
Founders, Hoxton Mini Press

This page: Club Mexicana (no.35)
Opposite: The Gate (no.31)

This page: Apricity (no.26)
Opposite: Holy Carrot (no.28)

This page: The Gate (no.31)
Opposite: Holy Carrot (no.28)

THE BEST PLACES FOR...

Brunch

Awaken your tastebuds with mallow's (no.23) tangy thali brunch or hearty-yet-healthy full English – both crowned with a satisfying dollop of scrambled tofu. Or head to Dauns (no.22) for a mid-morning smörgåsbord of Danish smørrebrød (open sandwiches) and fika-worthy sweet pastries.

A date

Stoke your romantic glow at Kin + Deum (no.25) with aromatic Thai curries and tasty small plates. Or get cosy at Koya (no.32), where you can slurp delectably thick noodles and steamy soups shoulder-to-shoulder at the intimate bar.

Special occasions

A chic setting and considered menu of elegant home-grown eats make Apricity (no.26) a superior supper spot. Or, if you're really looking to impress, splash out on Pied à Terre's (no.34) lavish 10-course vegan tasting menu and full wine pairing.

Family gatherings

The Gate (no.31) is great for the whole family – wild mushroom risotto cake for grandpa and filled courgette flowers and polenta chips for the little nieces. Nem Nem's (no.38) Vietnamese menu is full of crowd-pleasing dishes, from crispy spring rolls to pho noodle soup.

A junk food fix

Go for the mouth-watering Reuben sandwich and a generous portion of perfect fries at Rudy's Dirty Vegan Diner (no.37). Missing your fish 'n' chip fix? Sutton & Sons' (no.46) banana-blossom dupe is convincingly close to the real deal.

Catching up with friends

A vibrant setting, sharing-friendly taco menu and moreish margheritas make Club Mexicana (no.35) perfect for spontaneous social events. For a vegan mozzarella-fuelled catch up, Purezza (no.42) has your back with their crusty, generously topped pizzas.

Coffee (or tea) and cake

Enjoy a scrumptious peanut butter coffee and a big selection of sweet treats on the comfy sofas at WAVE (no.12). Or head to Brick Lane's Vida Bakery (no.5) for a slice of their signature six-layered rainbow cake and a pot of tea.

Convincing non-vegan friends

Chow down on some dumplings, bao and spicy dan dan noodles with a beer or two at Facing Heaven (no.19). If you fancy Indian, SpiceBox's (no.20) Chick'n Korma and Shroom Keema will have the most die-hard meat eater converted to the joys of plant-based eating.

1

PHO

Fresh Vietnamese street food

VEGAN FRIENDLY

When hunger hits hard in the busier parts of town, this nationwide chain is there like a reliable old friend. Their menu is full of vegan dishes that taste like the main event, rather than an afterthought. Choose from huge bowls of steaming noodle soup, topped with plentiful sprigs of fragrant herbs, or a hearty plate of aromatic, mushroom-topped fried rice seasoned with lemongrass and chilli. The cosy interiors feel secluded and relaxed, whether you're with friends or just having a quick lunch between errands. Grab a rich and sustaining enoki and shiitake pho to power you through the rest of your day – or night.

163–165 Wardour Street, W1F 8WN

Nearest station: Tottenham Court Road

Other locations: multiple, see website

phocafe.co.uk

2

MILDREDS

International menu in a smart setting

VEGAN

Mildreds is a beloved staple of the London veggie scene, having served up a globe-trotting array of dishes from their original Soho location for over 30 years. Today Londoners are blessed with beautiful branches across the city, so wherever you are there should be delicious plant-based fare in reach. If burgers are your thing, the fasolia patty with aioli and red shaata is a must. Otherwise, try some starters to share: daikon gyoza, Roman-style artichoke panelle, harissa home fries. You may not be in for a culinary epiphany but with its elegantly ingredient-led menu, Mildreds can be counted on to deliver consistently grown-up food.

45 Lexington Street, Carnaby, W1F 9AN
Nearest station: Oxford Circus
Other locations: multiple, see website
mildreds.co.uk

3

PILPEL

Fresh, authentic, quality falafels

VEGAN FRIENDLY

Sometimes all you want is some perfect falafel – crispy and hot, with plenty of creamy houmous and that satisfying crunch of tangy veg. But, as most people know, this deceptively straightforward vegan staple can all too easily go wrong. Inspired by the Tel Aviv falafel stand run by the founder's grandad, these falafel-filled pitta are always spot on – authentic, delicious and served by friendly staff. If you're ever remotely peckish near a Pilpel branch – they're dotted around east London and the City – then just join the fast-moving queue. The old man would definitely approve.

5 Queen's Head Passage, Pasternoster Row, EC4M 7DZ
Nearest station: St Paul's
Other locations: multiple, see website
pilpel.co.uk

4

CROSSTOWN

Moreish doughnut and coffee shop

VEGAN FRIENDLY

If you haven't already discovered this New York-inspired chain of sourdough doughnuts then you're in for a lemon-thymey, peanut-buttery glazed treat. The Marylebone branch is exclusively vegan but all Crosstown shops and stalls, from Canary Wharf to Broadway Market, carry an extensive vegan range. Their minimal black-and-white interiors draw attention to the long glass cabinet filled with a tempting display of doughnuts glistening with jewel-like icing – all waiting to be chosen (the hard bit) before being devoured (easy).

5–6 Picton Place, W1U 1BL
Nearest station: Bond Street
Other locations: multiple, see website
crosstowndoughnuts.com

CROSSTOWN

vegan
CROSSTOWN
5-6 picton place
VEGAN
CROSSTOWN
DOUGHNUTS
CROSSTOW
CROSSTOWN
vegan doughnuts
& specialty coffee

DOUGHNUTS

5

VIDA BAKERY

Spellbinding gluten-free bakery

VEGAN

You may not have realised it, but your life could well have a half-foot-high, rainbow-layered, cake-shaped hole in it right now. Luckily you can fill it fast, down on Brick Lane. Invite your best friend or your on-trend mother, and whisk them to this pastel-coloured haven for all things sweet, vegan and gluten-free. Next, choose a hot drink, served in cute mismatched mugs, and succumb to the sugar-induced euphoria. Not someone with a huge sweet tooth? Go for a cupcake, with its perfect ratio of icing to cake.

139 Brick Lane, E1 6SB

Nearest station: Shoreditch High Street

vidabakery.co.uk

6

MOTHER

Canalside café, juice bar and takeaway

VEGAN

Stroll through Hackney Wick and you'll find MOTHER near the banks of the River Lea – where on sunny days customers spill out into the Olympic Park, clutching takeaway tacos and toasties. Lovingly conceived by three siblings, this is the local spot to gather at communal wooden tables for nourishing all-day breakfasts, fruit-topped pancakes and smoothies, or linger over açai bowls while watching canal boats glide past. For those in a hurry, MOTHER has a small-but-brilliant kiosk just outside Hackney Central station. Grab a cold-pressed juice and dairy-free croissant to go.

Unit 1, Canalside, Here East Estate, E20 3BS

Nearest station: Hackney Wick

Other location: Hackney Central

mother.works

HOW TO SHOP IN OUR
PLASTIC FREE PANTRY
1. WEIGH JAR
2. WRITE THE
WEIGHT ON IT
6. TAKE TO THE TILL
ASK THE TEAM

7

FLAT EARTH PIZZA

Planet-friendly pizzeria

VEGAN FRIENDLY

Dough devotees, prepare yourselves: this Hackney pizza palace is about to turn your world upside down with its deliciously different, (mostly) plant-based creations. And when we say your world, we also mean the world. Not only are Flat Earth's toppings infinitely more exciting than the ones you'd find at your average pizzeria, they're also much kinder on the planet, with plenty of local veg, tangy ferments and foraged ingredients finding their way onto your faultlessly chewy base (which, by the by, is made using heritage grains). Order the Hackney Hot – a fiery fusion of jalapeños, hot salsa and pickled beetroot that's perfectly tempered by creamy Young Vegans mozzarella and guaranteed to make you melt.

286–289 Cambridge Heath Road, E2 9DA
Nearest station: Cambridge Heath
flatearthpizzas.com

8

BUBALA

Small plates, big flavour

VEGAN FRIENDLY

That it offers a vegan tasting menu titled 'Bubala Knows Best' is all you need to know about this acclaimed Middle Eastern restaurant. Take its word for it and devour a seemingly endless parade of tasty morsels: simultaneously tender and crispy aubergine, intricately spiced batata hara, inexplicably meaty mushroom skewers and chunky houmous scooped up with fluffy laffa pillows. Sit at the emerald-green bar, where you can sip on zesty orange wine while you gorge, before finishing (no matter how stuffed you think you are) with a creamy coconut malabi. Mezze-merising.

65 Commercial Street, Spitalfields, E1 6BD

Nearest station: Aldgate East

Other location: Soho

bubala.co.uk

BUBALA

9

ALTER

Plant-based pan-Asian eats

VEGAN

Alter, as its name suggests, is big on doing things differently. Founded by chef Andy Goodwin to challenge misconceptions around plant-based food, Alter isn't a 'vegan restaurant' so much as just a really great one – whatever your culinary predilection. Its menu is just as colourful as its joyful canary-yellow walls, defying clichéd notions of what vegan food should look like with nutritious morsels of pan-Asian deliciousness. Everything on the menu is heavenly but if you must narrow it down, go for the small but mighty kung-pao crackers, creamy khao-soi noodle laksa and the seemingly misplaced but actually completely necessary pizza-dough 'horns'. Nope, we wouldn't alter a thing.

First Floor of Leman Locke, 15 Leman Street,
Whitechapel, E1 8EN
Nearest station: Aldgate East
alterldn.com

10

PLATES

Sophisticated dining with focus on nutrition

VEGAN

It's hard to talk about Kirk Haworth's dishes without first mentioning what spectacular works of art they are, but this crafty chef is not overly preoccupied with aesthetics. Kirk's high-end concept is built on a sustainable menu of nutritious dishes devised to be as curative as they are tasty – devoid of meat, dairy, gluten and refined sugar, and bursting with plant power. Dishes change with the seasons, but highlights include a delicate seaweed caviar-topped potato and pea fritter, and an outright masterpiece of a main that marries cabbage, mushrooms and teriyaki tempeh with a jammy red wine sauce. It all looks far too beautiful to eat, and yet somehow tastes even better than it looks.

538 Kingsland Road, E8 4AH
Nearest station: Dalston Junction
plates-london.com

11

LA FAUXMAGERIE

Artisanal plant-based cheese shop

VEGAN

You can't miss this stylish take on the traditional cheesemonger, appropriately located on Shoreditch's Cheshire Street. Pop in and you'll find a moreish and tangy almond-based Brixton Blue (authentically aged with the same mould responsible for making Stilton and Gorgonzola so distinct) and a delightfully gooey truffle-infused 'Camemvert'. If you are new to the fledgling world of artisan vegan cheese, let the apron-clad experts guide you through their many UK-made offerings. Just don't blame us if you end up going back to pick up more 'Mozzarisella' sooner than you thought.

20 Cheshire Street, E2 6EH
Nearest station: Shoreditch High Street
lafauxmagerie.com

12

WAVE

Imaginative dishes in a peaceful space

VEGAN

Follow the WAVE sign on Mare Street down an inconspicuous alley to this plant-adorned space. In warm weather you can sit out in the courtyard; otherwise, sink into one of the sofas or have a gentle swing on a hanging chair. Order a peanut butter coffee (you read that right – and yes, it's unbelievably good) and get perusing an all-day brunch menu that's sure to get your mouth watering. Perhaps a salted caramel shake? Or a stack of caramelised banana pancakes? If you prefer your treats savoury, the zalmon bagel with dill and watercress, marinated mushroom roll or tofu scramble will do nicely.

11 Dispensary Lane, E8 1FT
Nearest station: Hackney Central
weareveganeverything.com

13

BLACK CAT

No-fuss hearty meals

VEGAN

Anyone who's been vegan or veggie for a while will enjoy a sense of nostalgia at this workers' cooperative in Lower Clapton. Their generous portions of homecooked curries, pies and lasagne have inspired a following of loyal and happy regulars. The seasonal menu changes every week but you can be sure to find a selection of sandwiches (from seitan steak to smoky tempeh) as well as Caribbean stews and nourishing soups. The library of activist titles, posters and evening events hint at the café's anarchist spirit, while the unpretentious decor and communal tables guarantee that everyone feels welcome.

76A Clarence Road, E5 8HB
Nearest station: Hackney Downs
blackcatcafe.co.uk

14

ANDU CAFÉ

Ethiopian BYOB café

VEGAN

Some places become part of your routine for simple reasons – at this humble café, the combination of tasty, affordable food, great location and the option to bring your own drinks to kick off a night out, goes a long way. Fading 90s Ethiopian travel posters and knick-knacks cover the walls and the menu has pretty much just one offering, the sampler platter, made to perfection. Fuel up on the berbere lentil stew and other delicately spiced vegetable dishes, all mopped up with squidgy injera bread, before heading on to one of the many nightspots nearby.

528 Kingsland Road, E8 4AH
Nearest station: Dalston Junction
anducafe.co.uk

15

THE VURGER CO.

Indulgent burgers and shakes

VEGAN

Napkins at the ready – you'll need them when tucking into a jaw-dislocatingly tall Vurger, along with skin-on fries and the unsurprisingly decadent Oreo shake. The stars of the show here are the patties, some made from beans and veggies, others from Beyond Meat or 'chicken', all doused in a range of rich condiments laid on so thickly that you may require more napkins still. Both branches give you the option to buckle down with your burger *al fresco* – in an outdoor seating area at the Shoreditch branch, or a quick escalator ride up to Jubilee Park in Canary Wharf.

6 Richmix Square, Cygnet Street, E1 6LD

Nearest station: Shoreditch High Street

Other location: Canary Wharf

thevurgerco.com

16

LOVE SHACK

Patch of paradise in a railway arch

VEGAN

Blink and you might miss this small settlement – seemingly built from driftwood and rush matting – nestled up against busy Cambridge Heath station. This former wasteland has been revived by three old school friends into a makeshift, desert-island-chic getaway complete with a beach bar, deckchairs and hammocks – so you won't even notice you're sipping your piña colada next to the A107. Go all out and order the chimichurri quesadilla with pica de gallo salsa, plus a side of oyster mushroom buffalo wings – but don't forget to ask about upcoming events, so you catch some live music or stand-up comedy before hopping on the train home.

Arch 298, 299 Cambridge Heath Road, E2 9HA
Nearest station: Cambridge Heath
loveshackldn.com

17

HORNBEAM CAFÉ

Delicious, non-profit community café

VEGAN

Even if you're not a Walthamstow local, this café is one to watch. Many vegan food talents, like Spicebox (no.20), cut their teeth in residencies here. Volunteer-built as an environmentalists' centre in 1994, Hornbeam is deep-rooted in the local community and hosts a wide range of events, from herbal medicine workshops to Afro-Brazilian drumming for kids. When there is no residency, volunteers prepare pay-as-you-feel meals using locally-sourced ingredients that would otherwise go to waste. Keep an eye on their social media feeds to find out who the next food star will be.

458 Hoe Street, E17 9AH
Nearest station: Walthamstow Central
hornbeam.org.uk

18

SILO

Eco-chic dining

VEGAN FRIENDLY

You might assume that the world's first zero-waste restaurant is fully vegan. It isn't, but then Silo is full of surprises (the on-site laundry, the lamps made from mushrooms and intriguingly cryptic menu). And anyway, there are enough plant-based offerings to make up a tasting menu so long you'll wonder if it will ever end – not that you'll want it to. Sure, the vegetables themselves are humble by anyone's standards, but Silo's chefs are remarkably skilled at magicking the likes of even the simplest potato into enticing purées and porridges – something they'll do before your very eyes if you take a seat at the bar. Just don't ask where the bin is.

Unit 7, Queen's Yard, Hackney Wick, E9 5EN
Nearest station: Hackney Wick
silolondon.com

19

FACING HEAVEN

Innovative Chinese small plates

VEGAN

This new successor to chef Julian Denis' cult Sichuan hole-in-the-wall Mao Chow is bigger and, yes, even better than the original. It's lively, cheek-by-jowl and sometimes downright raucous atmosphere will remind even the most disaffected Londoner why they fell in love with Hackney in the first place. Sit yourself at a bright yellow table and get ready for an onslaught of bold and layered Sichuan-pepper-fuelled flavours. Umami-rich dan dan noodles, crispy oyster mushroom bao, the chef's secret blend of 'meaty veg' and the Hong Kong-style French toast, will all have you scrambling to visit again. Bring non-vegan foodie friends who need wowing.

1A Bayford Street, E8 3SE
Nearest station: London Fields
facing-heaven.com

20

SPICEBOX

New-generation curry house

VEGAN

Stroll down Walthamstow's Hoe Street to find this contemporary spin on the British curry house. On the menu, you'll find old favourites like bhaji, samosas, jalfrezi and korma, but not as you might know them. Flavours are layered and natural, with crunchy, fresh textures that perfectly balance sweet, savoury and, of course, spice – try the jackfruit vindaloo with a cooling raita or a chana chaat with spiced chickpeas. Come at night and the vibrant colour-blocked dining room may have you feeling like you've stumbled into a Varanasi alleyway after a particularly strong bhang lassi. Bring on the banana chai doffle.

58 Hoe Street, E17 4PG
Nearest station: Walthamstow
Other location: Leytonstone
eatspicebox.co.uk

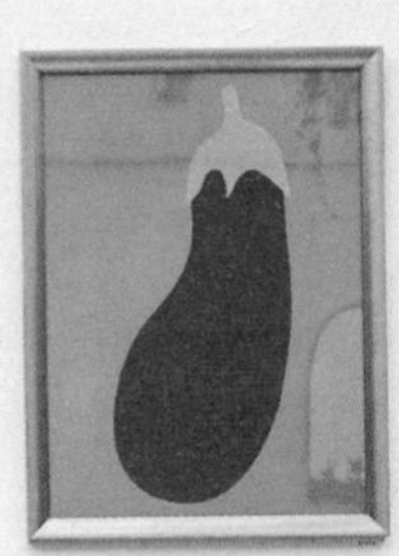

21
UNITY DINER

Non-profit restaurant serving tasty classics

VEGAN

Brainchild of vegan campaigner and social media star Ed Winters, this is the place to head if you want to explore the East End while also funding a good cause (all profits go to Surge Sanctuary, an 18-acre sanctuary with over 100 rescued animals that the team behind the diner helped to set up). Take your pick from a menu filled with old favourites – burgers, tofish and chips, mac 'n' cheese and fully loaded salads – and join the lively conversations under the 'The Future is Vegan' neon sign.

60 Wentworth Street, Spitalfields, E1 7AL
Nearest station: Aldgate East
unitydiner.co.uk

22

DAUNS

Scandi comfort food

VEGAN

Rickard Daun is the proud owner of the only bricks-and-mortar Scandi-vegan deli in London – and proud he should be. The Swedish chef's lovingly homecooked menu is a veritable smörgåsbord of comfort-food joy, whether you're grabbing a light lunch of seitan roast and horseradish mayo-topped smørrebrød (open sandwich) or craving something more substantial, like classic creamy 'meat' balls and fluffy mash laced with lingonberry jam, or even a saucy flatbread-wrapped tunnbrödsrulle (hot dog) smothered in Swedish mustard and Danish ketchup. Make like a Swede and prep your palate with a spicy shot of Akvavit between courses. Skål!

77 Wentworth Street, E1 7TD
Nearest station: Aldgate East
dauns.co.uk

Cafe & Deli
Scandinavian Vegan

23

MALLOW

Global food with local focus

VEGAN

Like its 'mother' restaurant, plant-based stalwart Mildreds, mallow's menu is confidently international. But far from biting off more than it can chew, this elegant plant-based newcomer manages to hit the mark with every cuisine it dishes up, from flawlessly spiced Thali brunch spreads to piquant pibil tofu tacos and criminally indulgent mushroom croque monsieurs. What's more, it's as devoted to sustainability as it is flavour, with the bulk of ingredients sourced from hyper-local suppliers, including neighbouring Borough Market. Waste is kept to a minimum in the kitchen – and on your plate, if you know what's good for you.

1 Cathedral Street, Borough Market, SE1 9DE
Nearest station: London Bridge
mallowlondon.com

24

CAFE VAN GOGH

Friendly non-profit café

VEGAN

An iron sign at the leafy end of Brixton Road welcomes you to this community-run space, just round the corner from the house where Vincent van Gogh lived during his brief sojourn in London. The chairs and tables (along with plenty of plants, books and paintings) look like they were thrifted from former trattorias and assembly halls and create a whimsical backdrop for long conversations over hearty moussaka, followed by an energizing affogato. The café works with local charities to provide opportunities for young and vulnerable people, which means that every bite really is as good as it tastes. Don't miss the famous Sunday roast.

88 Brixton Road, SW9 6BE
Nearest station: Oval
cafevangogh.co.uk

25

KIN + DEUM

Modern Thai cooking

VEGAN FRIENDLY

At the point just before London Bridge turns into buzzing Bermondsey, you may spot what looks like a cosily lit living room. Feel free to enter and join a lovely family affair where a sister and brother team of second-generation Thai restaurateurs merge traditional recipes with their flavoursome take on Bangkok street food. Glass noodle broths, fragrant tom kha and aromatic green curry – all the crowd-pleasing dishes and flavours are here, in fresh-tasting, unpretentious but quietly brilliant form.

2 Crucifix Lane, SE1 3JW

Nearest station: London Bridge

Other locations: King's Cross, Soho, Camden

kindeum.com

26

APRICITY

Thoughtful feasting

VEGAN FRIENDLY

Consideration is king at lauded chef Chantelle Nicholson's stylish Mayfair restaurant, where genuine concern seems to run through every inch of the operation – be it agonising over supply chains, fretting about food waste or just ensuring employees get home at a reasonable hour. Meat and veggie options dwarf the plant-based ones, but don't let that deter you – the tangy miso-roasted cabbage, delicate red butterhead salad and juicy summer oyster and black pearl mushrooms are easily the tastiest things on the menu, along with an unexpectedly delectable dip made from kitchen leftovers. Apricity even extends its hospitality to diners' dogs. So thoughtful.

68 Duke Street, Mayfair, W1K 6JU

Nearest station: Bond Street

apricityrestaurant.com

27

TENDRIL

Unfussy plant-based plates

VEGAN FRIENDLY

Tendril dubs itself a '(mostly) vegan kitchen', which might come as a relief to those whose friends and family are (mostly) flexitarian. That said, plants are very much the stars of this refreshingly unpretentious show, in which meaty mushrooms lead the main course, tasty tostadas come piled with crunchy veggies and vegan tiramisu feels as indulgent as its dairy equivalent. The set 'discovery' menus don't necessarily showcase the best options so carve your own path à la carte and go for the bolder plates with the biggest flavours.

5 Princess Street, W1B 2LQ
Nearest station: Oxford Circus
tendrilkitchen.co.uk

TENDRIL

28

HOLY CARROT

Virtuous dining

VEGAN

With a cocktail menu inspired by the occult and a signature dish called Sexy Tofu, this Knightsbridge hotspot might not sound like the most pious of haunts, but wellbeing disciples should have a little faith. It's gluten-, sugar-, additive- (and, of course, animal-) free recipes are nothing but saintly. Take a pew in the heavenly dining room – all white marble tables and dried-flower arrangements suspended like celestial clouds – and nourish body and soul with fluffy purple potato croquettes, tender palm-heart 'calamari' and oyster mushroom buffalo 'wings', followed by a wickedly good miso caramel sponge cake. Divine.

Urban Retreat, 2–4 Hans Crescent, SW1X 0LH
Nearest station: Knightsbridge
holycarrot.co.uk

29

FARMACY

Organic farm-to-table restaurant

VEGAN

Earthy meets glamorous in this much-hyped Notting Hill destination, a bright, wood-bedecked space where hand-thrown pots and rattan sit alongside designer furniture and expensive hairstyles. Living up to its name, Farmacy is all about the health-promoting potential of plant-based food, infusing a long, detailed menu with produce from its own biodynamic Kentish farm. Everything from the falafel waffles to the mushroom-based Farmacy benedict – not forgetting the CBD-infused mock- and cocktails – tastes as good as it makes you feel.

74–76 Westbourne Grove, W2 5SH

Nearest station: Bayswater

farmacylondon.com

30

EGERTON HOUSE HOTEL

Posh afternoon tea with all the trimmings

VEGAN FRIENDLY

Don your glad rags and head to luxury boutique hotel Egerton House for a full-blown high tea experience that's vegan (as long as you don't mind the sight of pampered pups enjoying their 'doggy afternoon tea' – not vegan). The window seats in the restful, cream-coloured drawing room are the perfect setting to contemplate tiers of sandwiches, scones with clotted coconut cream and delicate pastries, brought to you by the impeccably attentive butler – with a big pot of fine tea, of course. Don't forget to book in advance, they'll need at least 24-hours to prep all those sumptuous vegan treats.

17–19 Egerton Terrace, SW3 2BX
Nearest station: South Kensington
egertonhousehotel.com

31

THE GATE

World cuisine in a modern setting

VEGAN FRIENDLY

In 1989, two young Iraqi-Indian-Jewish brothers opened one of London's first vegetarian restaurants in rented space in a community centre. And so, The Gate Hammersmith was born. Now, many awards later and with locations in Islington and Marylebone, The Gate's tried-and-tested global menu will suit most occasions – whether you're eating with grandma, business clients or a group of friends. Start with the beetroot and mascarpone mousse, followed by the wild mushroom risotto cake and save some space for tiramisu.

22–24 Seymour Place, W1H 7NL

Nearest station: Marble Arch

Other locations: Islington, Hammersmith

thegaterestaurants.com

32

KOYA

Unpretentious Japanese canteen

VEGAN FRIENDLY

A queue snakes out the door of this cosy Soho noodle spot every lunchtime – and that's probably all the impetus you need to join the back of it. And if you're wondering if their limited vegan offer is worth the wait, it is. The udon (Koya's speciality) is chunky, chewy and delicious served both cold with a creamy sesame dip, and steaming hot in a comforting broth with mixed seaweed, pairing splendidly with tangy small plates such as the umeboshi (salted plums) and otsukemono (pickled vegetables). Bar-side seating and a buzzy but relaxed vibe make this an ideal spot for a quiet solo lunch or a casual date – just try not to dribble too much down your chin if it's the latter.

50 Frith Street, W1D 4SQ
Nearest station: Tottenham Court Road
Other locations: City of London, Broadway Market
koya.co.uk

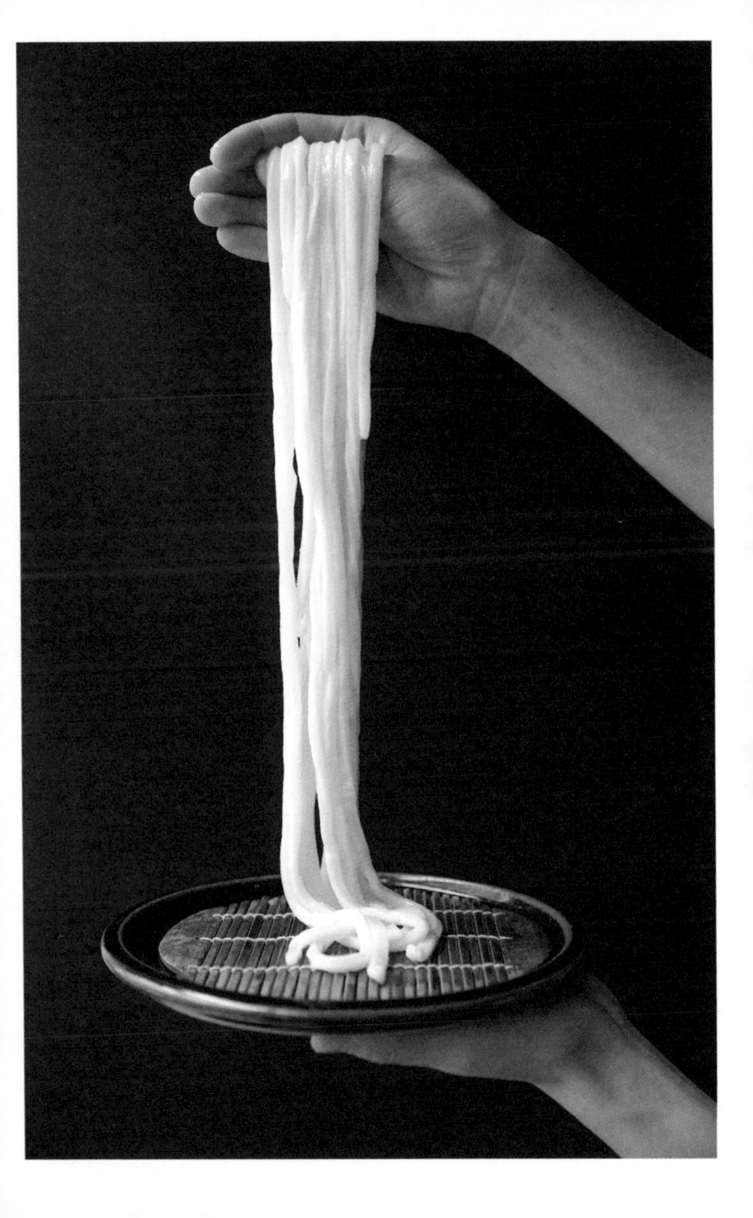

Koya-Ko, Broadway Market

33

GREENBAY

Vegan supermarket

VEGAN

It might sound like an auction site for vegetables, but this unassuming corner shop is – believe it or not – the UK's first and only fully vegan supermarket. Founded in 2015, this oversized larder of cruelty-free delights stocks more than 1,200 hard-to-find plant-based products, from bougie meatless dog food to tinned faux fish, vegan beauty products and a seriously impressive selection of dairy-free cheeses. Not planning a trip to Fulham any time soon? Greenbay offers same-day delivery inside the M25, so you could be polishing off that gelatine-free gourmet wagon wheel quicker than you think.

228 North End Road, W14 9NU
Nearest station: West Brompton
greenbaysupermarket.co.uk

GreenBay

34

PIED À TERRE

Flawless fine dining

VEGAN FRIENDLY

Should you ever get the chance to sample the 10-course vegan tasting menu at London's longest-standing Michelin-starred restaurant, for God's sake drop everything you're doing and take it. Exactly what goes on in the kitchen of this Fitzrovia favourite, from which deliciously surreal morsels of beetroot meringue, baked soybean terrine and chocolate mousse emerge, is anyone's guess, but we suspect chef Asimakis might be some sort of sorcerer. Opt for the all-out wine pairing – flawlessly matched by head sommelier Chanel Owen – and wake up the next morning wondering if the whole thing was just the loveliest dream you've ever had.

34 Charlotte Street, Fitzrovia, WIT 2NH
Nearest station: Goodge Street
pied-a-terre.co.uk

35

CLUB MEXICANA

Tantalising vegan tacos

VEGAN

With its neon-pink decor and complete refusal to serve food that's anything less than a full-on rave in your mouth, this Cali-Mex-inspired street-food spot is as bold as vegan dining gets. Order like you mean it, starting with layers of juicy plant mince, zesty pico de gallo and gooey 'cheese' on a bed of crunchy homecooked nachos, followed by as many tacos as you can fit in your belly – and if you suspect that might be less than the full menu, opt for the fried chick'n and cheeseburger varieties. Temper all that heat with a frozen margarita – or however many you deem necessary.

Ground Floor, Kingly Court, W1B 5PW
Nearest station: Oxford Circus
Other location: Seven Dials Market
clubmexicana.com

CHEEZE
BURGER
BBQ RIBS
Club
Mexicana

36

VEGAN PLANET

Authentic plant-based Chinese

VEGAN

The team behind Camden's gone-but-not-forgotten Dou Dou have created another plant-based Chinese utopia in this lively restaurant, located just around the corner from the original all-you-can-eat buffet. While regular Chinese menus can be a vegan nightmare due to the lack of choice, this one is for the exact opposite reason. It's replete with all manner of faithful classics – all in plant-based form. Begin with the 'prawn' toast and Peking 'duck' pancakes (both so close to the real thing you'll wonder if there's been some kind of mistake) followed by the tongue-tingling kung pao 'chicken' with Sichuan peppercorns and fiery sliced 'beef' so hot it almost hurts. Well worth it though.

11 Parkway, Camden, NW1 7PG
Nearest station: Camden Town
veganplanetuk.com

37

RUDY'S DIRTY VEGAN DINER

American-style fast food

VEGAN

Bury your face in Rudy's famous Reuben sandwich – a stack of finely sliced seitan-pastrami within generously dressed rye bread – and be transported to a roadside diner somewhere along a Pennsylvania highway. In reality you may be dodging TikTokers and sightseers in Camden Market, but Rudy's provides a hospitable pitstop with every friendly greeting and overflowing paper box. Come for the Reuben, stay for the cashew cheesy fries and Rudy's banana split. This is fast food that you'll want to savour.

Unit 729–731, Camden Stables Market, NW1 8AH

Nearest station: Camden Town

rudysvegan.com

38

NEM NEM

Inventive Vietnamese cuisine

VEGAN FRIENDLY

From the outside, it might look indistinguishable from countless other Vietnamese restaurants in London. But it's long been at the forefront of the plant-based revolution, offering a dedicated (and extensive) meat- and dairy-free menu. You can find everything from fresh summer rolls to dip in fragrant green sauces and restorative bowls of steaming pho, as well as vegan updates on classic dishes like chicken with cashew nuts and duck curry. The menu is far too long to get through in just one sitting, so you might find yourself making a lot of return trips to Islington. Not your neck of the woods? They've just opened a sister restaurant, Nom Noms, on the Kingsland Road.

279 Upper Street, N1 2TZ

Nearest station: Highbury and Islington

Other location: Hoxton

nemnoms.co.uk

39

THE FIELDS BENEATH

Craft coffee and wholesome café food

VEGAN

When the owner went vegan in 2017, so did his coffee shop. Since then, dairy-free lattes and croissants, as well as slabs of mum's banana bread have lifted this Kentish Town West railway arch to new heights. Their new head chef has recently introduced a rotating menu of inventively tempting hot dishes and wraps, including a Korean BBQ with crispy fried onions. A daily fixture for many locals, The Fields Beneath has the lived-in feel of your best friend's kitchen – except here there are monthly wine tastings, five different kinds of plant milk in the fridge and a trusty coffee machine that whirrs into action at 7.30am.

52A Prince of Wales Road, NW5 3LN
Nearest station: Kentish Town West
thefieldsbeneath.com

40

CRAVING

Asian-fusian artisan café

VEGAN FRIENDLY

This local hotspot supplies south Tottenham with its quota of oat flat whites and charcoal sourdough toast, as well as inspiring pop-ups and sustainable interior design. Stop by for the delectable Asian-fusion dishes like hoisin jackfruit banh mi and roast dengaku aubergine, but stay for the lively and friendly atmosphere. Making the most of their new location in Ten87 Studios (home to over 150 recording artists), they now host regular DJ sets or live music on Thursday evenings. So you can hear the latest tracks from up-and-coming artists while you dine on vegan-friendly fare or linger over one of their speciality martinis.

39B Markfield Road, N15 4QA

Nearest station: Seven Sisters

craving.london

41

PLANT CLUB

Gluten-free Italian

VEGAN

That it's buried inside a multi-use space makes it worryingly easy to wander past this magical place – so easy in fact that a sign outside reads "yes, we are here" to stop you from missing it altogether. Once securely seated at one of the airy dining room's marbled tables, order a convincingly creamy vegan burrata, followed by the perfect plant-based margherita – generously topped with a rich tomato sauce and cashew-based 'notzarella'. We don't know if it's the impossibly light GF dough or the fact that Plant Club's chef is a proper Italian, but these are easily some of the best pizzas in London – vegan or otherwise.

49 Green Lanes, Newington Green, N16 9BU
Nearest station: Canonbury
plantclub.uk

42

PUREZZA

Rustic, family-friendly sourdough pizzas

VEGAN

Grab a few friends and cosy up in a wood-panelled booth in what feels like the contemporary offspring of a long lineage of pizzerias. Hit the pizza end of the menu and, regardless of dietary choices, everyone will be delighted by the blistered sourdough crust loaded with an up-to-date choice of toppings. Melty, in-house-produced brown rice mozzarella with roasted aubergines, wild forest mushrooms or BBQ pieces all hit the spot. All under-10s get free pizza, so there's no better place for a boisterous family lunch.

43 Parkway, NW1 7PN

Nearest station: Camden Town

purezza.co.uk

#plantpioneers
Purezza

43

AUN

Japanese-fusion restaurant

VEGAN FRIENDLY

A small slice of Japan bringing *wakon yosai* (a harmonious blend of Japanese sensibilities with Western techniques) to Stoke Newington Church Street. Inspired by traditional Japanese bars serving drinks and small plates to Tokyo's office workers, you're sure to find deceptively simple and delicious dishes here. The colours are muted, the menu down-to-earth yet inventive – try the five course vegan menu and savour delicately flavoured soy mince udon noodles and flavoursome furofuki daikon dipped in miso sauce. Wash it all down with a glass of sweet plum wine or sake served in handmade, *wabi-sabi*-style ceramic cups.

178 Stoke Newington Church Street, N16 0JL

Nearest station: Stoke Newington

aun-restaurant.com

土佐鶴
純米
上等酒
純米酒
純米酒
土佐鶴

AUN
Japanese Tapas Restaurant

44

CARAVAN

Antipodean-inspired fusion dining

VEGAN FRIENDLY

Caravan, with its industrial interiors and casually excellent menu, is all about effortless style. These restaurants – six of them, at the last count, but each with their own individual character – have a relaxed set-up, with creative, globally-inspired and health-giving mains like the aubergine bhaji served with shaved fennel and coconut yoghurt or charred sweet potato with spiced black bean salsa. They are strong on plant-based options, although there's more available at lunch than brunch. Try the spacious and popular King's Cross branch for dinner and drinks (they have a stellar cocktail list) or the more intimate, original Exmouth Market location for a midweek catch-up.

1 Granary Square, N1C 4AA
Nearest station: King's Cross St Pancras
Other locations: multiple, see website
caravanrestaurants.co.uk

45

WHAT THE PITTA

Not-so-dirty kebab house

VEGAN

Get ready for a superhero version of that late-night guilty pleasure: the döner kebab. In this clean, stainless-steel-shiny space just off Camden High Street (with locations on Brick Lane and Croydon BOXPARK, too), you can marvel at the uncanny familiarity of it all while knowing that the only 'meat' in your meal is perfectly spiced soya strips. Add crunchy salad, addictively creamy sauce – and perhaps some onion rings on the side – and you're all set. One regret? They stop serving at 10pm, which doesn't help when you're hit by a 4am kebab craving after a great night out.

89–91 Bayham Street, NW1 0AG

Nearest station: Camden Town

Other locations: Brick Lane, Croydon

whatthepitta.com

46

SUTTON & SONS

Classic chip-shop fare, but make it plant-based

VEGAN FRIENDLY

Tender flakes of cod encased in mouth-meltingly crispy batter must be a top contender for the rookie vegan's most-missed cuisine – and one of the hardest to replicate in plant form. Luckily this tiny chain of traditional chippies, however, has come pretty close to fooling us with its meaty banana-blossom fillet, which is marinated in samphire and seaweed for a convincingly oceanic flavour, before being tossed in a fluffy eggless batter and fried to perfection in groundnut oil. Other surprisingly realistic dupes include tender 'calamari' made from Japanese potato starch and a delightfully succulent 'scampi' made from shiitake mushrooms. Just make sure you ask for the vegan menu, so you don't order the real thing by mistake.

90 Stoke Newington High Street, N16 7NY
Nearest station: Rectory Road
Other locations: Hackney Central, Islington
suttonandsons.co.uk

SUTTON
SONS

CONTRIBUTORS

Sara Kiyo Popowa is a north London-based artist, recipe developer and photographer. Known as Shiso Delicious on Instagram, she is a keen advocate of plant-based food and a low-waste lifestyle and holds workshops and events in London and beyond. Sara is also the author of *Bento Power: Brilliantly Balanced Lunchbox Recipes*, which is inspired by her Swedish and Japanese heritage.

Emmy Watts is a Camden-based writer specialising in fun things to do in London with kids. She's been fully vegan for less than a year but in that time, she's eaten some of the best meals of her entire life (most of them while researching this book). Emmy has written three other books for the opinionated guide series, including *An Opinionated Guide to Eco London: Enjoy the City, Love the Planet.* She's slowly overcoming her aversion to aubergines.

Sam A. Harris is a travel and food photographer who lives in east London. He regularly shoots for *The Telegraph* and other publications, as well as directly with restaurants and chefs. Although most of the vegan food Sam tried was cold by the time he ate it, it still tasted pretty damn good.

Hoxton Mini Press is a small indie publisher based in east London. We make books about London (and beyond) with a dedication to lovely, sustainable production and brilliant photography. When we started the company, people told us 'print was dead'; we wanted to prove them wrong. Books are no longer about information but objects in their own right: things to collect and own and inspire. We are an environmentally conscious publisher, committed to offsetting our carbon footprint. This book, for instance, is 100 percent carbon compensated, with offset purchased from Stand for Trees.

INDEX

An Opinionated Guide to Vegan London

First published in 2019 by
Hoxton Mini Press, London
Second edition published 2022

www.hoxtonminipress.com

Text by Sara Kiyo Popowa and Emmy Watts
All photography © Sam A. Harris*
Copy-editing by Samantha Cook, Faith McAllister and Octavia Stocker
Design and sequence by Daniele Roa and Richard Mason
Production by Sarah-Louise Deazley

*Except for photographs The Gate (p.4, p.9) © The Gate 2022; Club Mexicana (p.5) © Nic Crilly-Hargrave Photography / Club Mexicana; Apricity (p.6) © Stefan Jansen Birch; Holy Carrot (p.7) © Joakim Blockstrom; Holy Carrot (p.8) © Lesley Lau; Alter (first and second images) © Nic Crily Hargrave; Alter (third image) © Emma McGettrick; Apricity © Paul Richardson; Bubala (all images) © Helen Cathcart; Caravan Club © Caravan Restaurants; Club Mexicana © Nic Crilly-Hargrave Photography / Club Mexicana; Craving © Craving; Dauns (first image) © Rickard Daun; Dauns (all other images) © Martin Usborne; Flat Earth © Aleksandra Boruch / Flat Earth Pizzas; The Gate © The Gate 2022; Greenbay © Greenbay; Holy Carrot (both images) © Joakim Blockstrom; Koya (first image) © Ola O. Smit; Koya (second image) © Anton Rodriguez; mallow (all images) © mallow London; Mildreds (all images) © Mildreds London; Pied à Terre © Claude Okamoto and Maurizio Leoni / OL Visual; Plant Club © Valentina Giora; Plates (first image) © Helen Cathcart; Plates (second image) © Tom Harrison; Silo © Matt Russell; Sutton & Sons © Bec Newman; Tendril (all images) © Amrita Diwanji; Unity Diner © Martin Usborne; Vegan Planet © Martin Usborne.

Compiled by Sara Kiyo Popowa, Emmy Watts and Hoxton Mini Press
With thanks to Matthew Young for initial series design

The content and information in this guide has been compiled based on facts available at the time of going to press. We strongly advise you to check each location's website before visiting to avoid any disappointment.

ISBN: 978-1-914314-31-5

A CIP catalogue record for this book is available from the British Library.

Printed and bound by OZGraf, Poland